LIGHTNING
BOLT
BOOKS™

Space Exploration Robots

Jackie Golusky

Lerner Publications • Minneapolis

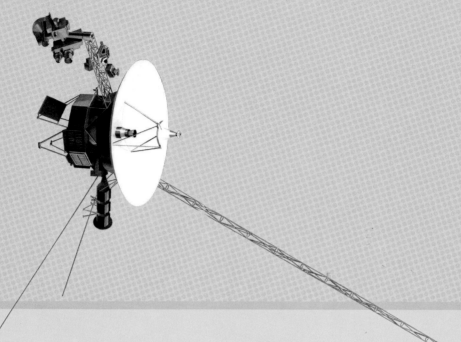

Lerner Publications Company
An imprint of Lerner Publishing Group, Inc.
241 First Avenue North
Minneapolis, MN 55401 USA

For reading levels and more information, look up this title at www.lernerbooks.com.

Main body text set in Billy Infant regular.
Typeface provided by SparkType.

Editor: Rebecca Higgins **Photo Editor:** Cynthia Zemlicka

Library of Congress Cataloging-in-Publication Data

Names: Golusky, Jackie, 1996-author.
Title: Space exploration robots / Jackie Golusky.
Description: Minneapolis, MN, USA : Lerner Publications, 2021. | Series: Lightning bolt books robotics | Includes bibliographical references and index. | Audience: Ages 6-9 | Audience: Grades 2-3 | Summary: "Robots are out of this world! Space robots go beyond where people can explore. Readers will meet robots orbiting other planets, exploring their surfaces, and much more"— Provided by publisher.
Identifiers: LCCN 2019049908 (print) | LCCN 2019049909 (ebook) | ISBN 9781541596962 (lib. bdg.) | ISBN 9781728413617 (pbk) | ISBN 9781728400464 (eb pdf)
Subjects: LCSH: Space robotics—Juvenile literature. | Space probes—Juvenile literature. | Outer space—Exploration—Juvenile literature.
Classification: LCC TL1097 .G65 2021 (print) | LCC TL1097 (ebook) | DDC 629.47—dc23

LC record available at https://lccn.loc.gov/2019049908
LC ebook record available at https://lccn.loc.gov/2019049909

Manufactured in the United States of America
1-47802-48242-2/12/2020

Table of Contents

Out of This World

A robot rockets deep into outer space. It's on a mission to explore where no human ever has gone.

The *Curiosity* rover has sensors that record the weather.

Robots carry out commands. Some of these machines explore space. They have sensors to understand their environment.

Scientists use strong metals and plastics to build space robots. These robots can survive the extreme temperatures of space.

Buoyant Rover for Under-Ice Exploration is tested in Antarctica's freezing waters.

Some robots look like humans. They have armlike parts that grab tools. Others look like cars, with wheels to drive across planets.

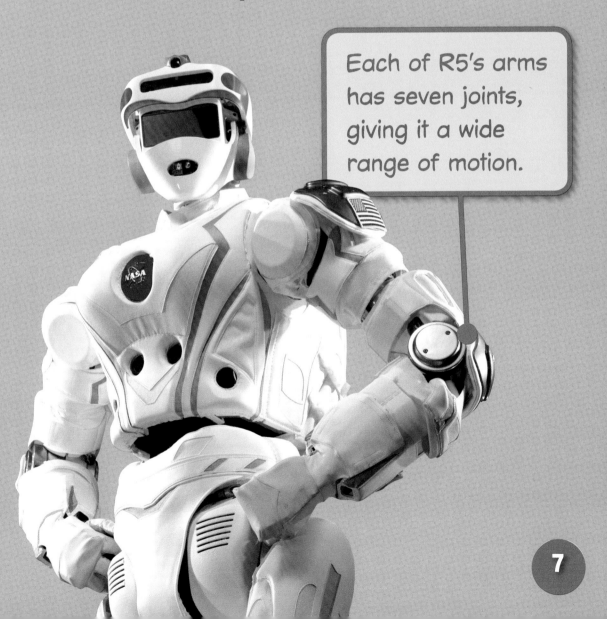

Each of R5's arms has seven joints, giving it a wide range of motion.

Space Probes

Probes fly to explore space. They study our solar system and land on planets.

Probes explored Saturn and Jupiter. One probe landed on Saturn's moon Titan. Another discovered Jupiter's rings.

One probe landed on Venus.
This planet is very hot. It is too
hot for people to explore.

Venus's surface
temperature is about
900°F (482°C).

Voyager 1 left our solar system in 2012.

Voyager 1 has flown very far away. It left Earth in 1977. In 2020, it was about 14 billion miles (23 billion km) from the sun. It helps scientists learn what is outside our solar system.

Helping Humans in Space

Some space robots have parts that look like human heads and arms. Astronauts use these robots to do hard jobs.

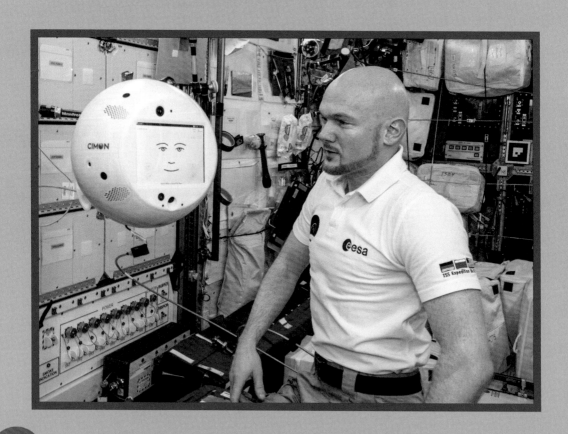

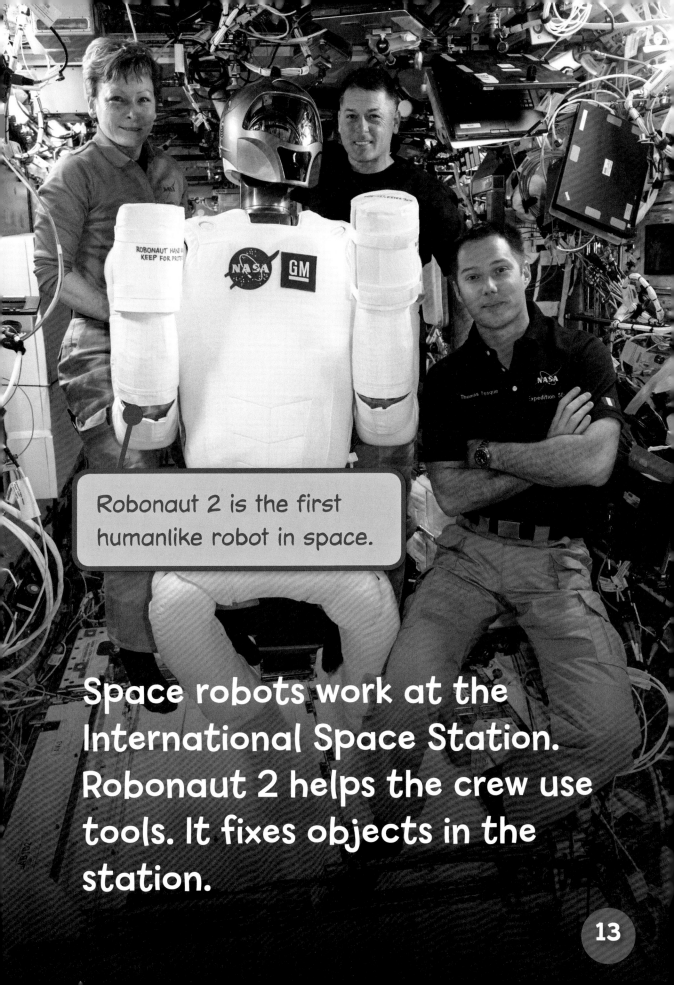

Robonaut 2 is the first humanlike robot in space.

Space robots work at the International Space Station. Robonaut 2 helps the crew use tools. It fixes objects in the station.

Robots also work outside the space station. Dextre's arms are 11 feet (3.4 m) long. These long arms hold tools.

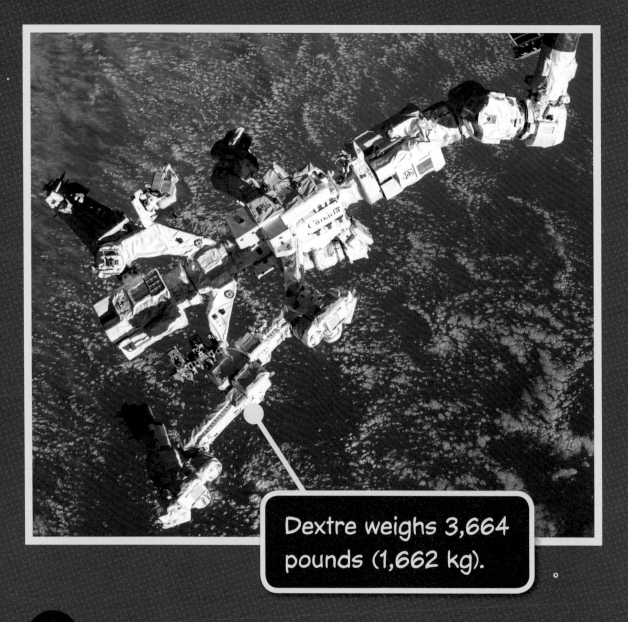

Dextre weighs 3,664 pounds (1,662 kg).

Canadarm2 grabs a spaceship.

Dextre gets help moving around. It rides at the end of the 58-foot (18 m) Canadarm2. This lets it work on different parts of the station.

Rovers

Rovers are space robots with wheels. Some are as small as a skateboard. Others are as big as a car.

Scientists use computers to steer rovers.

Rovers explore Mars. Scientists on Earth steer the rovers. The rovers drill into soil to gather data. They test the air. They also take photos.

This illustration shows *Curiosity* studying a rock with its laser.

New rovers carry tiny science labs. They fire lasers at rocks. Sensors measure the light that bounces back. Scientists use this data to learn what is inside the rocks.

Scientists will keep making space robots. New robots will go farther into space. They will do more jobs. They will help us learn more about outer space.

Robots help us understand our solar system and beyond.

Behind the Robot

Some scientists design probes in labs. Other scientists travel to the International Space Station to work on robots there. Scientists test robots before sending them into space. They use special machines to shake the robots to make sure they can launch and land without breaking.

Fun Facts

- One space probe carries pictures and sounds from Earth. Scientists sent the pictures and sounds in case aliens find the probe someday. The aliens could see and hear what Earth is like. The probe also has directions to Earth.

- The United States sent a pair of rovers to Mars in 2003. They were designed to work for ninety days. But one of them worked for more than ten years!

- The human-shaped robot on the International Space Station is strong. But it can also be used for delicate jobs. Its fingers are so gentle that they can pick up paper without crinkling it.

Glossary

astronaut: a person trained to work in space

crew: the people working on a ship or space station

International Space Station: a science lab that circles Earth. Sixteen countries helped design it.

laser: a narrow beam of light

sensor: something that senses heat, light, sound, or motion

solar system: the sun, along with the asteroids, comets, moons, and planets that circle around it

Further Reading

NASA: All about Venus
https://spaceplace.nasa.gov/all-about-venus/en/

NASA: Build Your Own Spacecraft
https://spaceplace.nasa.gov/build-a-spacecraft/en/

NASA: Mars *Curiosity* Rover
https://mars.jpl.nasa.gov/msl/spacecraft/rover/summary/

Schaefer, Lola. *Flying Robots.* Minneapolis: Lerner Publications, 2021.

Smibert, Angie. *Space Robots.* Minneapolis: Abdo, 2018.

Troupe, Thomas Kingsley. *Space Robots.* Mankato, MN: Black Rabbit Books, 2018.

Index

Photo Acknowledgments

Image credits: NASA, pp. 2, 11, 15; NASA/JPL-Caltech, pp. 4, 16, 17, 18; NASA/JPL-Caltech/
MSSS, p. 5; NASA/JPL, pp. 6, 10; NASA/Bill Stafford/James Blair/Regan Geeseman, p. 7;
Johns Hopkins University Applied Physics Laboratory/NASA, p. 8; Stocktrek Images/Getty
Images, pp. 9, 22; NASA/ESA, pp. 12, 13, 14; NASA/JPL-Caltech/T. Pyle (SSC), p. 19.

Cover: NASA/JPL-Caltech/MSSS.